AF211705

WESTLEY OSBERT

IMPROVE CONCENTRATION

The Ultimate Guide to Complete Concentration, Learn the Effective Techniques on How to Improve Your Concentration and Stay Focused to Fulfill Your Dreams

Descrierea CIP a Bibliotecii Naţionale a României
WESTLEY OSBERT
IMPROVE CONCENTRATION. The Ultimate Guide to Complete Concentration, Learn the Effective Techniques on How to Improve Your Concentration and Stay Focused to **Fulfill Your Dreams** / Westley Osbert – Bucharest: Editura My Ebook, 2021
ISBN

WESTLEY OSBERT

IMPROVE CONCENTRATION

The Ultimate Guide to Complete Concentration, Learn the Effective Techniques on How to Improve Your Concentration and Stay Focused to Fulfill Your Dreams

My Ebook Publishing House
Bucharest, 2021

TABLE OF CONTENTS

CHAPTER 1

AN INTRODUCTION TO THE POWER
OF CONCENTRATION

If only you could concentrate more, you could probably accomplish almost anything.

This might sound somewhat hyperbolic but it's true.

Ultimately, success often comes down to who is willing to work the hardest and the longest and if you put more effort into *anything* then you'll be more likely to succeed.

Imagine for a moment that you are a writer who earns $2 for every 100 words you write. That might not seem like much, but now imagine that you were able to write 25,000 words a day. *Now* you're earning a lot, right?

That's $500 a day!

In your job, you probably aren't paid based directly on your output but that doesn't mean that you can't achieve more by working harder or longer. Ask yourself this: how many hours of your working day do you *really* spend producing your optimal amount of output? For most of us, we only really work our very best for a couple of hours a day. The rest of the time we spend looking at e-mails, we spend surfing the web or we spend on Facebook.

Imagine if you had infinite concentration. Imagine if you could work *solidly* for the full eight hours. You'd accomplish more than the rest of your team put together and it would only be a matter of time before your salary reflected that. You'd never have to stay late and in fact you'd probably get to go home *early* a lot of the time.

It's not just in our careers where concentration really matters though either. In the rest of our lives concentration is equally important. Imagine how much better your relationship would be if you were always giving your partner your full attention. Imagine how much you'd improve as a parent if your mind wasn't on other things. Concentrating on what is going on around you even makes you more alert and more focused when you're out and about. This makes you better at responding to a crisis situation and is what the Special Forces call 'situational awareness'.

8

In other words, being able to concentrate on what matters and being able to stay focused at all times is the secret to doing more and to doing everything *better*.

How does that sound?

What is Concentration, Really?

This book, as you've probably guessed by now, is all *about* putting you back in the driving seat and giving you full, unflinching mastery over your mental faculties. Once you've read this book to its conclusion, you'll be able to harness the full power of your brain at all times and put your focus exactly where it needs to be.

To do this though, you're going to need to know what focus really is and what all that actually entails. That means we're going to delve very quickly into some neuroscience, which is going to serve as the basis for everything else you'll learn over the course of this book. Don't worry if any of it doesn't make sense – you don't actually need to understand it to take full advantage of the tips we'll be looking at.

Executive Control and the Salience Network

So what exactly happens in the brain when you concentrate? Actually, a number of things are at play.

Firstly, you have an increase in specific neurotransmitters such as dopamine, norepinephrine and acetylcholine. These are similar to hormones that are produced in the brain and which alter our mood, our memory and more.

The neurotransmitters associated with attention and concentration are called the catecholamine neurotransmitters and are similar to those produced during a 'fight or flight' response. When you have an abundance of these chemicals in the brain, it causes you to stay more engaged, to remember what happens better and to generally be more alert and switched on.

These neurotransmitters will be produced where they are needed and in the case of most tasks that require our concentration, that means the prefrontal cortex. This part of the brain contains the various different areas that are required for 'higher order' cognitive tasks that involve planning, memorizing and deep thought. In fact, this more specifically involves a 'network' of brain areas that are together called the 'attention network' or the 'executive control network'.

10

This change in neurochemical profile alters the action of the neurons (brain cells) in that region. These are all 'excitatory' neurotransmitters which means that they increase the amount of electrical activity (action potentials) among cells. Conversely, you also have 'inhibitory' neurotransmitters which include the likes of GABA and adenosine.

As neurons change their rate of firing, this alters the brainwaves in that region. When we're concentrating hard, this tends to result in beta waves in the prefrontal cortex. Caffeine also increases the amount of beta wave activity in the brain.

But how does our brain know that something is important and worthy of our attention? While the answer to this isn't fully understood, what we do know is that it involves another network of brain areas called the 'salience network' and which includes the anterior cingulate cortex.

Essentially, the salience network and the ACC allow us to identify something as important consciously and this then allows us to direct the executive control network to things that matter. In turn, this causes a flood of dopamine and norepinephrine and encourages the limbic system and hippocampus to move more of the experience into long term memory.

Interestingly, the salience network is also related strongly to motivation and the will to 'keep going'. Mice with their salience networks removed find themselves giving up much more quickly when looking for food in a maze and ultimately this seems to be what's responsible for the 'will to go on'.

Also interesting, is that our attention can be directed by either internal or external factors. For instance, if you decide that something is important and opt to focus on it, then this is called 'top down' attention and it will activate the brain across the *dorsal* attention network. On the other hand though, your attention can also be triggered by a noise or distraction in your environment which will cause you to switch your focus reflexively. In this case the information flows from the bottom up via the *ventral* attention network.

Confused yet? Don't worry. Just keep all this information roughly in your mind and we'll be looking at how it relates to some of the different strategies and techniques you can use to increase your focus and attention.

CHAPTER 2

FINDING YOUR TRUE MOTIVATION
SO YOU HAVE REAL GOALS TO PURSUE

So now you know what focus is, why it matters and how it works in the brain.

The next question is how you can make it work for you and maintain your focus as long as you need it on any given thing.

Most people unfortunately will go about this in entirely the wrong manner. That's because they are constantly trying to *fight* their natural inclination to pay attention to certain things and in turn they end up struggling to stay focused.

When you try and force yourself to focus on the Word document you're working on rather than on your Facebook page or whatever else is trying to steal your attention, you'll essentially be engaging your salience network and trying to actively *force* yourself to focus on that thing and block out the other distractions from the ventral attention network, or from the other activity firing in your brain elsewhere.

Something else to bear in mind here too, is that maintaining such intense focus is very tiring and actually requires a lot of energy. It's easy to become worn out as a result and to flag.

So what do you do instead?

Simple – you ensure that what you need to focus on is *genuinely* fascinating and engaging. To do this, you just have to find something that truly motivates you and that drives you.

If you manage to find something that really matters to you then you will have intrinsic motivation without even trying. In other words, your brain will produce the reward hormone (dopamine) automatically bringing your focus strongly to what you're doing.

Basically, when you struggle to stop looking at Facebook, it's because your brain finds Facebook *more rewarding* and more *salient* than what you're currently doing. The same goes for *Candy Crush Saga* or for YouTube videos of cats. After all – these things are all designed *to be* highly rewarding and almost addictive.

But if your job is more fascinating and more interesting than *Candy Crush* then you won't be tempted to bring it out of your pocket. Think about it: when was the last time you started playing *Candy Crush* at the movies, on a rollercoaster or at a concert featuring your favorite band?

Imagine if you enjoyed your work as much as your favorite band. Imagine if you enjoyed *everything* as much as your favorite band.

Now you'd be more focused and more present at all times and you'd live a richer and more rewarding life that resulted in better achievement.

Flow States and Startups

Another interesting neuroscience subject that relates to concentration is the 'flow state'.

A flow state is characterized as a state of mind where the individual experiences intense concentration and focus and where they are highly engaged with what they're doing. Today, researchers believe that flow states may behind many of the biggest breakthroughs and achievements in human history and it's believed that this is the most productive, efficient and effective mental state we can achieve.

Chances are that you may have experienced a flow state yourself…

Examples of Flow State

- When you're engaging in sports and the world almost seems to 'slow down' allowing you to react with perfect clarity and reaction speed.

- When you're deep in conversation and lose track of time – you check the time and realize that it's 3am.

- When you're so deep in work that you find yourself ignoring the need to go to the toilet or even get up to eat.

These are all considered flow states and they're all characterized by an increase in catecholamine neurotransmitters combined with a *decrease* in apid brainwaves. Rather than seeing beta waves, instead the brain goes into an alpha/theta wave state. At the same time, many areas of the brain actually *shut down* in what is known as 'temporohypofrontality'.

It's almost like meditation where every outside distraction is removed and you're completely focused on one thing – to the point where time almost loses its meaning.

What does this have to do with finding your passion? Simple: when you're working toward your passion, you are *in* a flow state at all times.

Studies show that most start-up companies are in better 'flow' than any other business. Why? Because they're excited

16

and passionate about their business and because they have an exciting, youthful energy.

And this is great news for those startups, because businesses with large amounts of flow actually produce far greater product than those without.

So if you learn to love what you do, you'll be in constant flow.

How to Love What You Do and Find Your Passion

If you're working in a boring office job, filled with people you don't like and in an environment you find uninspiring, then you won't be in flow and you'll struggle to concentrate. This is bad news.

The same goes if you're stacking shelves in a grocery store. Unless you're super-passionate about groceries, you're probably not in flow and you're probably not working optimally.

For these reasons, you *need to change your career* right now if you want to fulfil your potential. That means finding your calling – finding the thing that will motivate you to get up first thing in the morning. The thing that will cause that salience network to fire like mad.

Now a lot of people will say they can't do this – they have too many responsibilities and financial strains to just 'up and leave' their currentjob.

So here are some things you can do to start moving towards a career you truly love:

- Start looking for outside work while at your current job – you don't need to quit your day job until you've found your perfect position elsewhere. So there's really no risk!

- Alternatively, try starting a 'side project' from home in the form of a small business. You can create a blog, start selling a product etc. and then wait until it's earning enough money to support youwhen you love your current employment.

- Think about what it is that will truly make you excited:
  o Ask yourself when you last felt truly energized at work
  o Think about the jobs that your role models have
  o Think about what you love doing and all the ways that can be made into a career
  o Don't be afraid to combine jobs or think outside the box – there's nothing to stop you having a part time job *and* a small business venture!

- Visualize what success looks like to you and what happiness looks like to you. Now think about what steps you'd have to take to get there. What career would support this lifestyle?

18

CHAPTER 3

METHODS FOR MAINTAINING CONCENTRATION

No matter *what* your job entails though, there are going to be times when you're not feeling particularly motivated or when you're not feeling supercharged.

One tip then is to try thinking about what it is about your job that *is* exciting or at least motivating.

If you are currently working in a job that you find dull for instance, then remind yourself why it is that you're doing that work and how it can eventually lead to a better lifestyle. Perhaps you're working here in order to earn enough money to launch your dream business? Maybe you're working here to support your family. Focus on that fact and this will remind you why your job *matters* and why it's worth your full attention.

Creating a longer-term goal is a great way to do this. Even if your current career/lifestyle doesn't excite you, then think about what your long term goals are and find something to feel excited and passionate about.

CBT for Concentration

Those of you who have studied any psychology might recognize this as a form of 'cognitive restructuring'.

Cognitive restructuring is a technique from CBT, or Cognitive Behavioral Therapy. CBT meanwhile is a psychotherapeutic technique used to treat a range of conditions ranging from social anxiety, to phobias, to OCD.

Essentially, CBT works in two stages:

1. Identifying the negative thoughts that are leading to stress/maladaptive behavior (mindfulness, thought reporting)

2. Changing those thought processes using a range of techniques (cognitive restructuring).

So if you were afraid of speaking in public for instance, you would first use mindfulness meditation (listening to your own thoughts) and thought reporting (writing a journal of what you think just before speaking) and then see what negative thoughts were causing that anxiety.

It might be that you find yourself thinking things like 'what if everyone laughs at me?' or 'I might stutter' which of course is what then *causes* you to freeze and to perform badly.

Thus you use two tools called 'thought challenging' and 'hypothesis testing'. Thought challenging means that you challenge your beliefs and break them down to see if they're accurate. Are people *really* likely to laugh at you? Or will they be more likely to be sympathetic and polite and continue listening? Likewise, does it really matter if you stutter? Ultimately, you'll never see these people again and you never claimed to be an amazing speaker? Who cares!

This should hopefully help you to relax and thus avoid the stressful 'fight or flight response'. At the same time, you can also use hypothesis testing to actually *test* the theory. This might mean standing up to speak in front of a crowd and then *purposefully* stuttering. It's terrifying, but very quickly you'll learn that it really doesn't matter what happens – people are kind and you'll survive!

But CBT can also be used in the reverse manner. You can also use cognitive restructuring to tell yourself that something *is* important and to focus on the reason it really matters. Repeat this like a mantra – I *need* to keep working on this, if I work now I can rest later, this work will help me achieve my goals.

21

Focus on the emotions that drive you to keep going and put aside any negative thoughts like 'five minutes on Facebook won'thurt'. We all know that five minutes is *never* five minutes.

As soon as you start using these techniques, you can actually start to lead your brain state and force yourself to focus on the things that matter.

When you do this, you will come to believe that what you're doing is very important and as such, your brain will respond in kind by producing the necessary neurotransmitters to keep you engaged and alert. Other things – like *Candy Crush* – won't seem as important and thus they won't be able to distract you.

It's Your Perception That Counts

What CBT really teaches us is that it's our *perception* of a situation that really counts as far as the brain is concerned. It doesn't actually matter what we're doing or how important that is. What matters is how important we *think* it is.

Let's put it this way: if you were standing on top of a volcano as it erupted, this would cause you a lot of panic and your brain would react by producing tons of norepinephrine and epinephrine. This would trigger the 'fight or flight' response and your heartrate would increase, your focus would narrow and you'd feel highly stressed and scared.

Did the volcano cause this? No: your belief that you were about to be incinerated did.

If you were in the exact same position but you genuinely believed that you were invincible, then you wouldn't have the same fight or flight response. You'd be able to stand back and just relax while the lava erupted around you.

Of course you'd also die… but your neurochemical profile would be completely different.

If you can change your perception of events, then you can *control* the release of neurotransmitters, you can *control* the activation of brain areas and you can make sure you're in the perfect state of mind for whatever task awaits you. You can be more present and in the moment when you're with friends, more focused when you're working and more relaxed when you're thinking creatively and engaging your 'default mode network'.

If you perceive something as important, then you will believe it is important and your body will react accordingly.

More Tips for Maintaining Concentration

With all this brain discipline, you should now start to find that concentrating on what you need to is a little easier. Now you're working on things that you love and already find highly engaging and valuable and you're using cognitive restructuring to make sure that this importance stays right at the forefront of your mind at all times.

Now your brain chemistry and the activation in your brain should all be supporting a highly focused and engaged state.

But there are a few more things you can do as well to help yourself stay even *more* focused…

Listen to Music

Remember how your attention works in both a 'top down' and 'bottom up' manner? In other words, if you're deep in focus while working on an all- important project, you can still find your attention interrupted if there's a loud noise from somewhere else or if you start to pick up on a conversation that sounds interesting.

So to help yourself concentrate better, you really need to be able to block out those distractions and a great way to do that is by listening to some music while at the same time using noise cancelling headphones.

Also important is to use the right *kind* of music. There is some evidence to suggest that listening to music can actually 'entrain' brainwaves meaning that our brains become more active when we listen to faster music. Pick something with a rapid, steady beat then and you may work *faster*. Pick something more relaxed conversely and you'll be more likely to be creative and come up with more interesting and unique ideas.

Another tip is to try listening to music on loop. That might not sound very exciting but that's exactly the point – when we listen to the same sounds over and over our brain eventually becomes desensitized to them. This is why we don't get disturbed by a ticking alarm clock for instance.

Listen to the same non-vocal, up-tempo album on loop and it will eventually fade into the background leaving only your dorsal attention stream (at least for your ears). This is actually a technique that Matt Mullenweg, creator of WordPress, reportedly uses.

Caffeine

There's a reason that many of us start our day with a big cup of coffee. As it happens, caffeine is very effective for increasing energy *and* concentration.

Ever wondered how caffeine works? Essentially it works by blocking specific receptors in the brain, those receptors being the A1 receptors. This in turn prevents the inhibitory neurotransmitter 'adenosine' from affecting the brain, which means that we don't get as sleepy or tired. The lack of adenosine meanwhile causes an *increase* in general activity throughout the brain and that in turn leads to a surge of other catecholamine neurotransmitters such as dopamine and norepinephrine. Together, these enhance our focus and help us to concentrate longer and harder.

Struggling to concentrate first thing in the morning? Then try drinking some caffeine!

Removing Other Distractions

Meanwhile, you should also remove other distractions from your environment and especially those that try to tempt you away from your work.

One of the biggest distractions for many of us these days is the internet. Whether we're watching cat videos, browsing Facebook or checking email, the web *always* seems to offer something else to distract us and prevent us from paying attention.

Thus a great strategy when you *really* need to work is to shut yourself off. That means either unplugging the internet for a bit, or using a piece of software such as 'Freedom' which will automatically disconnect you for certain periods. Obviously, this doesn't work if you *need* the web to produce your work. But otherwise, you can use this in order to leave yourself with nothing to do but work.

And if your work requires you to use a specific piece of software – such as Word – then you may be able to go one step further even by *switching off your mouse*!

The same goes for removing the GameBoy from within reach, or that magazine. If it's guilty of robbing you of your time then cut it out.

Introducing the Right Distractions

You know what though?

It's impossible to *always* be fully focused. With the best will in the world, your brain is only capable of concentrating for so long before it gives up the ghost and that's why it's very important to introduce strategic breaks into your workload. We'll be looking at this more in the next chapter but for now we can keep it simple: use desk toys in order to keep yourself focused.

Desk toys are things like cats' cradles, small desktop rock gardens, or games of one player solitaire. These are the perfect distractions because they don't suck you in.

So when you need to take a micro-break and you look up from your computer, you now have something you can fiddle with or look at that *won't* end up steeling countless hours. This strategy works because it's better that you be distracted by a desktop toy for two minutes than you be distracted by a computer game for 30.

CHAPTER 4

MAKING A SCHEDULE

The techniques covered in the last chapter will help you to maintain your focus and your concentration for long periods but ultimately this is still very 'reactive' – you're still effectively fighting against the urge to break focus.

In other words, we can still do better. And one way you can accomplish this is going to be by setting yourself up for success at the start of the day by creating a schedule that will help you to stay on-task and to get the most done.

So how do you go about this?

Starting the Day

The first thing to do is to start the day with the right tasks.

And actually, this has a lot to do with how you *end* the day. A good tip you see, is to end your day by leaving one task at least incomplete. This might sound like the last thing you should be doing but in fact it can have a very positive impact. Why? Because when you leave a job unfinished, it creates a psychological imperative to finish it first.

We *hate* leaving jobs unfinished and if something is half done, this creates a big urge to finish working on it as soon as possible.

And this is incredibly valuable because once you *begin* your work; you'll find that it helps get you into the flow. Like starting your car, starting working is actually what takes the most effort and is the most difficult in many cases.

An alternative option is to complete a fun and easy task first. Again, this goes against what many of us think of as the smartest move – often we feel inclined to start by completing the most difficult and unpleasant task so it is 'out the way'. D this though and you'll often find you end up putting off getting started.

Instead, start with the fun and enjoyable job, and you'll be able to ease yourself in gentler.

Niggling Tasks

Another tip is to try and remove the most niggling and frustrating tasks from your schedule early on.

Let's say for instance that you need to call a client or a partner and have a difficult conversation about some work you're delivering late. Many of us will put this off continuously but in doing so, we actually only end up making life worse for ourselves. The longer you put off completing these tasks, the longer they're going to play on your mind and distract you from what you need to be doing.

Remember everything we discussed regarding the neuroscience of concentration. When you have these 'open loops' (as Tim Ferris calls them) you have lots of additional, small things pulling at your attention and directing it away from the bigger and more important tasks you need to be focused on.

Likewise, when you have lots of small things playing on your mind, it makes it impossible to get into a state of flow as you'll constantly be interrupted.

So close the open loops as quickly as possible and free up the maximum amount of mental energy to focus on single, big tasks for long periods. Call those clients; send e-mails and completely annoying little jobs. Then sit down with a cup of coffee and start focusing on the *big* stuff.

Zombie Work

What is 'zombie work'?

Zombie work is any work you need to do that doesn't require your full attention or at least doesn't require you to be highly focused.

Writing an e-mail for instance is *not* an example of zombie work. Why? Because that requires you to use the creative parts of your brain and to really focus on what you're doing. On the other hand, stuffing envelopes or doing data entry *are* examples of zombie work.

To put it another way: zombie work is anything you can do equally well with the TV on in the background.

This is actually a particularly useful type of work as it allows you to fill time when you won't have your full attention available. If you're tired first thing in the morning, or last thing at night and you really can't focus, then you can use your 'zombie work' to stay productive without taxing yourself. You can also strategically place zombie work in between your longer work projects to give yourself a bit of a chance to recover mentally. Or how about using it to make the most of time when you're going to be forced to multitask?

Setting Rewards

When you first get into work, what is the first thing you do? For a lot of people, the answer is that they check their emails to see if anything important has come through.

32

Again this sounds smart… but it's not a good idea.

Unfortunately, when you check emails as the first thing you do in the day, you'll set yourself up to be in a 'reactive' state rather than a proactive one. What's more, you'll be quite likely to end up spending tons of time on it.

And there's also a good chance that you'll end up checking the email *again* later. And again. And again.

Instead then, try turning your e-mail into a 'reward' for good work. Not only will this spur you on to work harder but it will also mean that you don't have lots of interruptions.

Let's say you have 10,000 words to write in a day. Tell yourself that you can only check your email after you've written 2,000 words. Want a cup of tea? That will be another 1,000 words. Want to check Facebook for ten minutes? That'll cost you 5,000 words.

Now, instead of wasting hours checking your email, browsing Facebook and making tea, you'll only do those things once you've written 8,000 words and you're almost finished. It makes a *huge* difference… so try it!

CHAPTER 5

DAY-TO-DAY CONCENTRATION ADVICE

Right at the start of this book, we said that focus could make you better at pretty much everything and help you to get more out of your life. Focus and concentration isn't *just* about working – it's about being more present, being more observant and being faster to react.

So how do you go about concentrating more in day-to-day life?

Rich environments

The great thing about flow research is that it's showing us more and more ways to be more engaged with the environment and more excited by what we do. There are plenty of ways you can increase flow and one of the most promising is simply to create more 'rich environments' to spend time in.

34

Simply put: if you're working in a grey cubicle at work, then your brain is going to shut down and go into autopilot. Conversely, if you work in an exciting, modern office, then you're going to find yourself feeling more inspired, engaged and interested in what you're doing.

This can be traced back to our evolutionary routes. Being in a novel environment back in the wild would have meant discovering a new area with new potential threats and new potential food sources – thus it paid to be more alert and more focused.

You can work better then by making richer environments but you can also be more engaged with life by making other environments richer and more exciting. Decorate your home with more interesting ornaments, with plants and with more colorful paint and wallpaper. Take different routes home when you walk back from work. Wear more colorful clothes. All of it will help you to be more awake and more engaged.

Find the Fun

When you play a computer game, you're essentially training your brain and learning.

And it's learning that the brain enjoys and that we find addictive.

Think about it: when you pick up a new game, you have to learn the controls, then you have to learn the rules and then you gradually get better. Each time you do well, you hear a satisfying sound and see a flash of light or a score to reward you.

Learning these new skills causes you to form new neuronal connections in your brain via something called 'brain plasticity'. At the same time, the reward tells your brain that this was a *good* performance and thus the connection strengthens. *This* is what's addictive about games.

So why is *actual* learning so boring? Why is work so boring? It's because it's repetitive, there's no instant sense of reward and there's little in theway of challenge.

So instead of just going through the motions, you need to find what's fun about your given situations or you need to *make* it fun. If you can turn earning into a game with lots of little rewards, then you'll find studying better. Instead of just walking to work the same way every day, why not challenge yourself to discover new routes, to cut time off without jogging, or to avoid the cracks. Sound childish? That's the point. Kids love childish activities because their brains are so plastic at that age as they

36

learn. If you keep making games for yourself, you'll keep learning and your brain will *stay* plastic.

Instead of getting bored tidying, why not turn it into a game by throwing the rubbish into the dustbin from a distance and keeping a score as you go?

Making it Interesting

If what you're doing can't be made fun, then perhaps it can be made interesting.

This is the same thing as we mentioned before – it's staying switched on to the long term, disconnected benefits of the situation.

Let's be honest, sometimes it can be boring hearing our other half drone on about work. But to be a better partner, we need to stay focused. So remind yourself why it matters and why it's important. It matters because it will make you a better partner and if you're a better partner, you'll have a happier life. Or think about how it's interesting: perhaps the social dynamics are more illuminating than you at first give them credit for? What does your partner's mood tell you about *them*?

Likewise, if you're forced to read something dull, try and find what's interesting about it. If you need to do a project on door locks for your degree, then try to find *some* kind of passion for that subject. Think about it: door locks are essentially a type of cryptography, as expressed by a mechanic. If you like computers, then maybe think about how door locks relate to cyber security. There's always *some* angle you can use to make a subject more interesting.

CHAPTER 6

RE-GAINING CONCENTRATION
WHEN YOU LOSE IT

Hopefully all this advice is helping you to stay more focused and alert and to be more present and engaged no matter *what* the activity. But you're still going to need a contingency plan for when things go wrong. When you lose concentration, *then* what do you do?

Take a Break

Remember, concentration takes energy and most people agree that there is only a finite amount of time that it's possible to stay highly focused and productive.

What do you do once your concentration is broken, or you find yourself starting to flag and run out of steam?

One answer is to take a time out and to give yourself a break. If you try and 'force' yourself through this difficult point then in all likelihood you will either perform sub-par work, or to just waste time.

In fact, there are very few things *worse* than 'half working'. As the old adage goes: walk or sit, don't wobble!

Instead of trying to force yourself to work, give yourself some legitimate time off to recharge and spend that time eating or just relaxing, either for a brief five minutes or for a longer hour.

Brain Fuel

This is something that you hear a lot less often than you should: if you're running out of focus and struggling to concentrate, then you need to eat.

Remember: keeping that salience network at work and avoiding distractions takes a ton of mental energy. Eventually, that energy runs out and you're left with low inspiration and your brain running slowly. Fuel up with some carbs and you'll be able to dive back in and carry on working.

Here's something else to consider: certain foods and supplements can be very effective at helping you regain mental

40

energy. One example of this is coconut oil. Coconut oil encourages the liver to produce more ketones, which are an alternative source of energy (alternative to glucose) which the brain prefers for some tasks. Additionally, coconut oil contains a special type of fat called MCT (medium chain triglycerides) which the body absorbs immediately, thus providing instant energy instead of taking an hour to be absorbed by the blood stream.

Other foods and supplements can provide a boost in energy over the longer term – one example is omega 3 fatty acid which improves 'cell membrane permeability'. In other words, it makes the cell walls more permeable, thereby improving communication between cells. Another example is l-carnitine, which makes the cells more efficient at converting glucose into ATP (usable energy). The same also goes for lutein, CoQ10 and numerous other supplements. Vitamin B6 meanwhile gives you the building blocks to make lots of useful neurotransmitters. Creatine helps us to recycle *used* ATP (ADP and AMP) back into more ATP.

Many of these nutrients can be found in your diet though. So once your energy flags, eating is a crucial way to get it back. Staying hydrated is also *super* important.

How to Power Nap

If this hasn't helped you to regain your focus, then what might is a power nap. A power nap is one of the most effective tools in your arsenal when it comes to regaining and maintaining concentration. The secret is to make sure that you sleep for less than 40 minutes, which will ensure that you don't enter 'deep sleep' If you do sleep more than 40 minutes, then you need to make sure you go all the way to 90 minutes, in which case you'll be able to wake up after one complete cycle.

CHAPTER 7

LONG TERM ADVICE FOR KEEPING CONCENTRATED AS YOU APPROACH YOUR GOALS

Much of what we have discussed is about focusing in the short term on work or what you're doing. Really though, concentration is most powerful when it is maintained over time. What *really* counts is the ability to stay focused on your goals and work *day in and day out* on making them happen.

Break Your Goals Down Into Steps

One tip to do this is to break your goals down into smaller tasks. Want to lose weight? Don't set the goal of reaching '5 stone in 1 year' because it's just too distant and too out of your control. Instead, set the goal of exercising 4 times a week for one year. The weight will take care of itself but the goal you have is much easier to control and much more instantly

43

rewarding – remember what we said about getting that constant dose of dopamine as you get rewarded for hard work?

Break your goals down into smaller steps and it will be much easier to use the CBT techniques we discussed earlier to stay focused on them.

Training Your Concentration

Thanks to something called 'brain plasticity' – which we touched on earlier - the brain is able to adapt its shape and size depending on how we use it.

If you spend lots of time playing the cello for instance, then the area of your brain in the motor cortex responsible for fine finger control will *grow* over time. New connections will form between neurons and the connections you already *have* will become thicker.

Likewise, if you spend lots of time concentrating, guess what happens? You train your concentration and that gets bigger too. Very possibly, this would result in an increased size for your anterior cingulate cortex, which would also result in better motivation.

Conversely though, if you are constantly switching between tasks and you never concentrate for more than a couple of minutes, your ability to concentrate will atrophy. This is one of the biggest dangers of the technological world we live in – if you are constantly using your phone or going from one social media site to another, then you'll find your ability to concentrate wanes.

Don't worry if you're not a master of concentration just yet. The key thingis that you keep at it – in which case you'll get better as your brain develops. Practice concentrating at every opportunity and engage in tasks that require focus. If you do this enough, you'll eventually develop the necessary areas of your brain and you'll become masterful at it.

Mindfulness

We earlier discussed mindfulness as a part of CBT used to identify the contents of your thoughts. Actually though, mindfulness can also be a more general term that describes a type of meditation where you become more mindful of your own body, mind and environment.

Studies show that practicing mindfulness or any kind of meditation, can help you to be more present in the moment *and* to have a better long-term focus. If you want to step-up your mental game, then give it a go! Why not try the Headspace app?

CHAPTER 8

CONCLUSION

So there you have it: a ton of different strategies you can use to increase your focus and your concentration at work and in life, in the short term and in the long term.

We covered some in-depth neuroscience and looked at how concentration in the brain works – but we also distilled that information into some actionable tips and steps you can use yourself.

It's a lot to take in though – so in case you weren't *concentrating* let's recap with some take-home points:

• Concentration is the result of dopamine and norepinephrine, along with the action of the salience network to direct our attention to what we deem important.

• Concentration takes energy. To be effective you need to recognize this and try to manage that energy, either by accepting the ebbs and flows in your workload, or by fueling yourself with power naps, snacks and breaks.

• We automatically concentrate on the things we find most interesting, engaging and rewarding. Instead of forcing yourself to engage with something dull, it's often easier to change the nature of the work or your lifestyle!

• Find something you're passionate about and you'll be in a constant state of flow, resulting in more happiness, more focus and more productivity!

• Then again, you can often find the fun or the fascination in even the dullest tasks – you just have to look for it!

• Remind yourself *why* you're doing something. Break your goals down into steps and focus on your end game to power through the monotony.

• Remove outside distractions, use desk toys and music and unplug from the web for a bit.

• Practice concentration – it *can* be trained!

• Meditation has been shown to improve concentration and flow.

- Create a more engaging and 'rich' environment for work and relaxation.

- Practice cognitive behavioral therapy to take control of your thoughts.

And with that, you're ready to start taking control of your brain and mastery of your concentration. Once you focus, you'll find that everything becomes easier and the whole world becomes more colorful and rewarding.

Printed by Libri Plureos GmbH in Hamburg, Germany